SMART CHARTS

WEATHER

By Madeline Tyler

BookLife
PUBLISHING

©2019
BookLife Publishing
King's Lynn
Norfolk PE30 4LS

ISBN: 978-1-78637-455-4

Written by:
Madeline Tyler

Edited by:
Holly Duhig

Designed by:
Daniel Scase

PHOTO CREDITS

WEATHER

SMART CHARTS

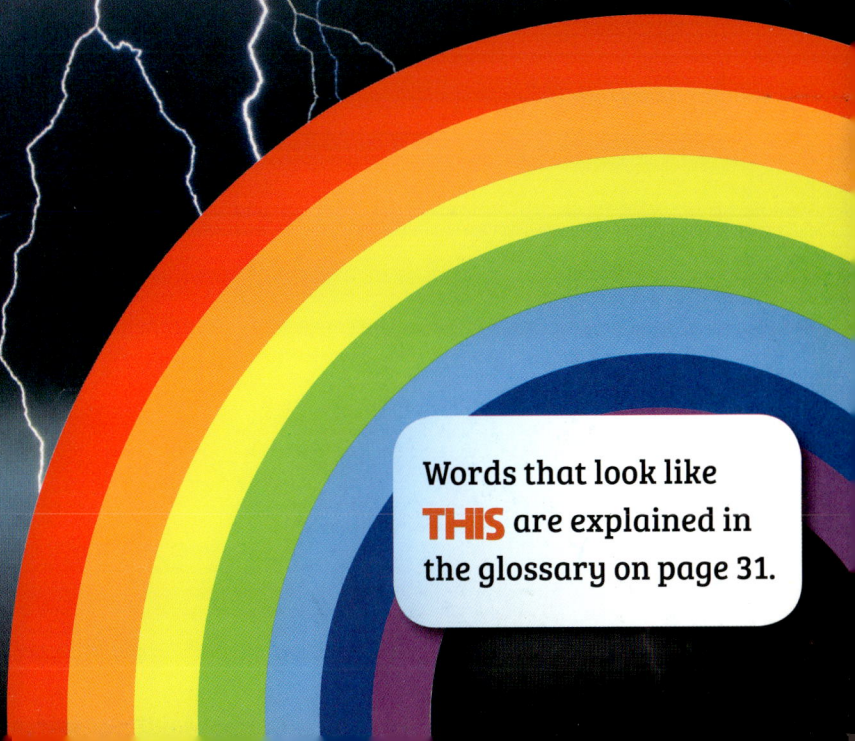

Words that look like **THIS** are explained in the glossary on page 31.

KNOW YOUR CHARTS!

WHAT IS DATA?

Data is another word for information. Data can be facts, numbers, words, measurements or descriptions. For example, someone might collect data about the different types of houses along a street. They might record how many houses there are, what colour they are, and when they were built. Data can be hard to understand, or **INTERPRET**, especially if it's a long list of words or numbers. Putting the data into a chart or graph can make it easier to read. Different charts and graphs are used to show different types of data.

TABLES AND TALLY MARKS

Tables are used to write down data about different things. They are usually quite simple and have a few rows and columns. Tally marks are used to count things up. The tally marks can be recorded in a frequency table. This shows how many of each thing there are. Tally marks are drawn in sets of five to make them easier to count. You draw four lines and then the fifth one strikes through the others.

HOUSE COLOUR	TALLY	TOTAL
RED	⦀⦀	6
BLUE	|||	3
GREEN	||	2
BROWN	⦀⦀ |||	8
YELLOW			1

PICTOGRAMS

You can use the data from a frequency table to make a pictogram. Pictograms show the same information but with pictures or symbols.

RED	🏠🏠🏠	6
BLUE	🏠🏠	3
GREEN	🏠	2
BROWN	🏠🏠🏠🏠	8
YELLOW	🏠	1

KEY: 🏠 =2

Bar charts usually show data that can easily be split into different groups, such as colours or months. It is easy to compare the data in a bar chart to see which column is the highest.

BAR CHARTS

y-axis NUMBER OF HOUSES

Red | Blue | Green | Brown | Yellow

x-axis HOUSE COLOUR

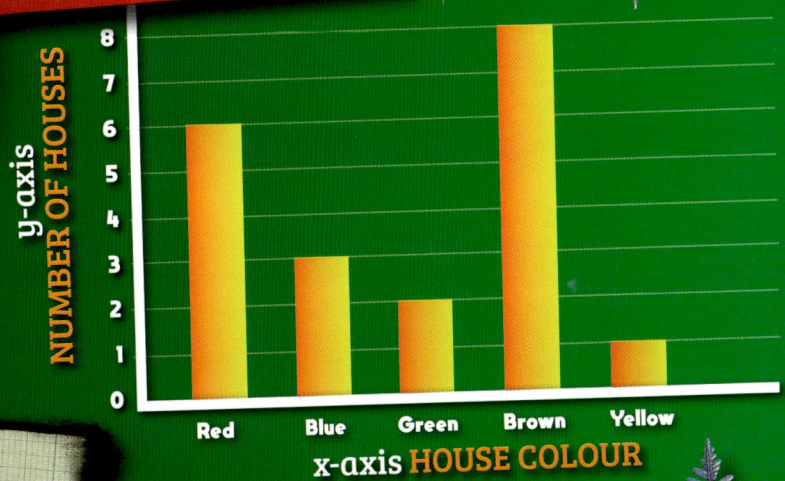

Graphs have two axes. The one that goes up and down is the y-axis and the one that goes left to right is the x-axis.

PIE CHARTS

10%
15%
40%
30%
5%

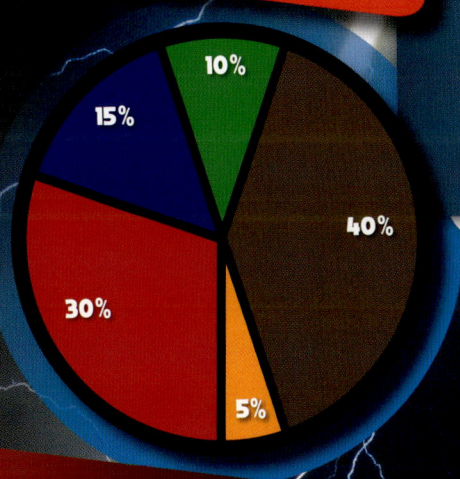

Pie charts are usually circular. They are split into different slices, just like a pie! Pie charts show data compared to the total number of something. For example, the total number of houses on the street is 20. Two of the houses are green – this is ten percent (10%) or one-tenth (1/10).

LINE GRAPHS

Line graphs show if there is a correlation (a connection or trend) between two sets of data. This line graph shows that there is a **POSITIVE CORRELATION** between the number of houses and time – the number of houses has increased as time has passed.

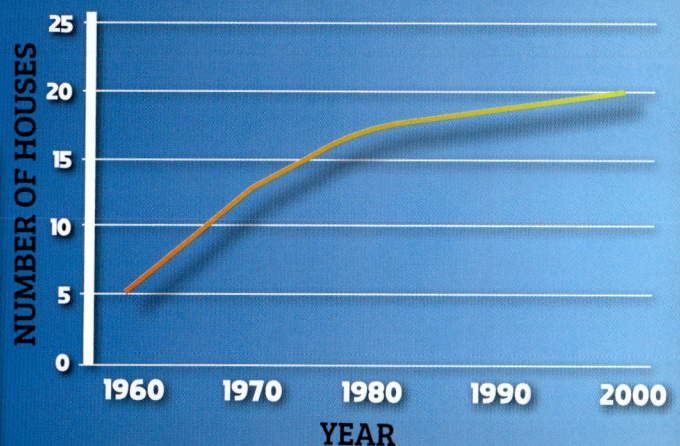

NUMBER OF HOUSES

1960 | 1970 | 1980 | 1990 | 2000

YEAR

WEATHER

Sometimes it's sunny outside, and other times it might be cloudy. It might rain a lot one day, but not at all on another day. It might get so cold in the winter that it snows for days and days without stopping, while in the summer it might be so hot that fires catch and spread through forests and fields. These are all different types of weather. The weather can be warm or cold, sunny or cloudy, dry or wet. Thunderstorms, lightning, hail and wind are all types of weather too.

Most of the time, the weather is quite **PREDICTABLE**, and we can use weather forecasts to see what the weather will be like over the next few days. This helps us to know what kind of clothes to wear, and whether we'll need to pack an umbrella or a sun hat.

WHAT CAUSES THE WEATHER?

Weather on Earth is caused by heat from the Sun and moving air in the **ATMOSPHERE**. The Sun warms up a layer of **GASES** low down in Earth's atmosphere. The warm air rises, and the cool air sinks. This moving air is called wind. Wind can clear away clouds to bring clear skies, or it might blow clouds in to bring rain or snow.

The Sun's warmth also turns **MOISTURE** from plants – and water from lakes, rivers and oceans – into water vapour in a process called evaporation. Water vapour is a gas which, along with nitrogen, oxygen, argon, carbon dioxide and a few other gases, makes up the air around us. Water vapour in the air can become clouds and fall back to Earth as rain, or even as hail or snow if it's cold enough.

The amount of moisture or water vapour in the air can affect how and where clouds form. Some clouds form very close to the ground; these are called mist or fog.

Visibility means how far, or how well, you can see. If you can see more than 180 metres (m) in front of you through the cloud, then it's mist. If you can't, it's fog.

CLOUD	VISIBILITY
MIST	MORE THAN 180 m
FOG	LESS THAN 180 m

CLIMATE

Climate is the **AVERAGE** weather that people can expect in a specific place, usually over a year. Different parts of the world have different weather patterns, which means that they have different climates. There are five main climate zones on Earth: tropical, arid, temperate, continental and polar.

- Tropical: warm and can be either dry or wet. Rainforests are part of the tropical climate zone.
- Arid: dry areas that can be cold or hot. Deserts are part of the arid climate zone.
- Temperate: the temperature is never too extreme, with **MILD** summers and winters that don't get too cold.
- Continental: mostly inland, far away from the sea. Most areas have hot summers and cold winters.
- Polar: found towards the very top and bottom of the world. Some areas experience winter all year round.

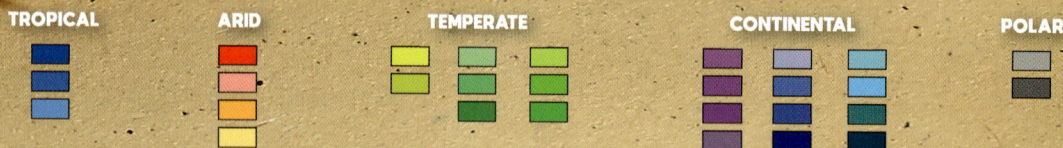

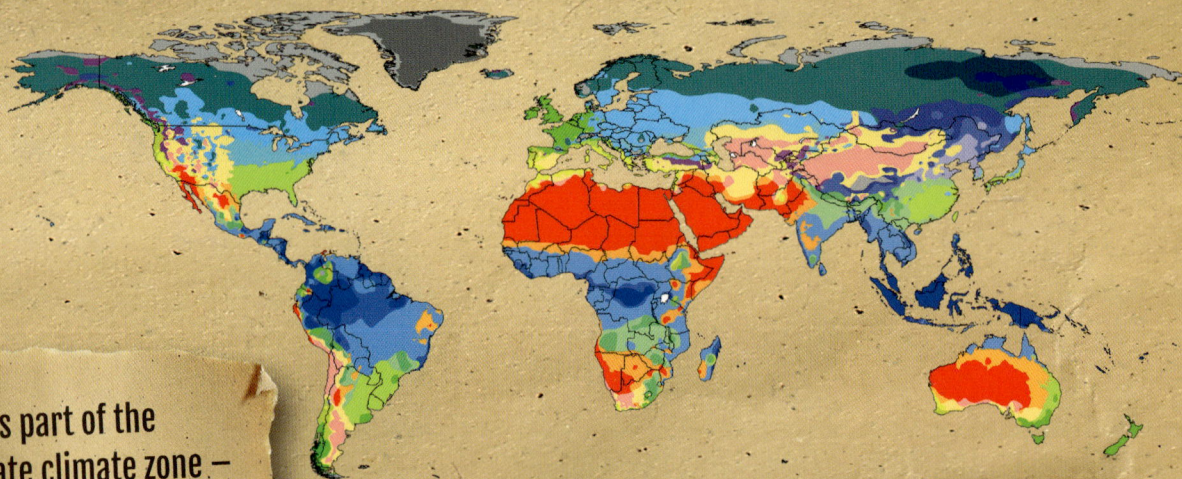

TROPICAL   ARID   TEMPERATE   CONTINENTAL   POLAR

The UK is part of the temperate climate zone – it has a temperate climate. Most of Brazil belongs to the tropical climate zone – it is home to the tropical Amazon rainforest.

This is a climate graph. It shows the average rainfall and temperature in parts of the Amazon rainforest in Brazil.

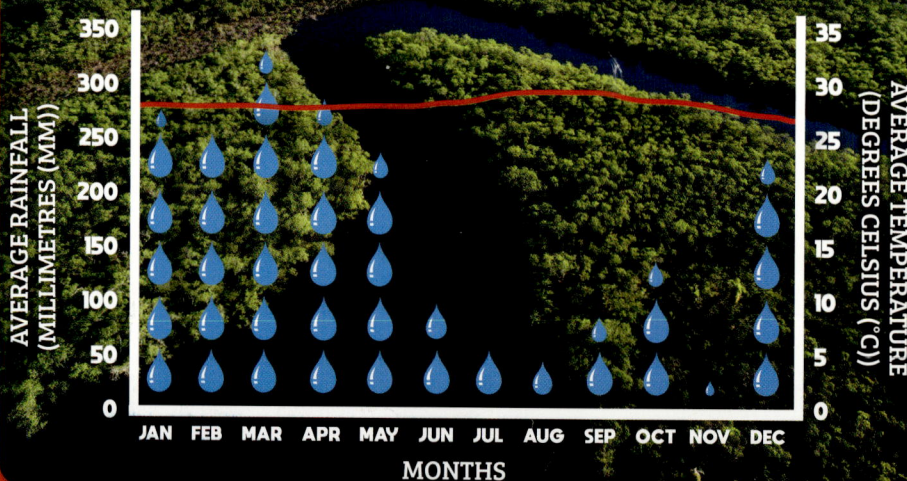

AVERAGE RAINFALL (MILLIMETRES (MM))

350
300
250
200
150
100
50
0

AVERAGE TEMPERATURE (DEGREES CELSIUS (°C))

35
30
25
20
15
10
5
0

JAN FEB MAR APR MAY JUN JUL AUG SEP OCT NOV DEC

MONTHS

SEASONS

Did you know that Earth doesn't sit upright? It's actually tilted to one side along its axis. Earth's axis is an imaginary line that runs straight through the planet, from the very top at the North Pole to the very bottom at the South Pole. Earth spins around its axis, which gives us night and day. Earth also has another imaginary line that runs around the middle of it. This is called the Equator. Everything above the Equator is the Northern Hemisphere, and everything below it is the Southern Hemisphere. As Earth orbits the Sun, the Sun will be shining more on either the Northern Hemisphere or the Southern Hemisphere at different times in the year. This is what gives Earth its seasons.

When the North Pole is tilting towards the Sun, it is summer in the Northern Hemisphere and winter in the Southern Hemisphere. This is between June and August. When the South Pole is tilting towards the Sun between December and February, it's the other way around!

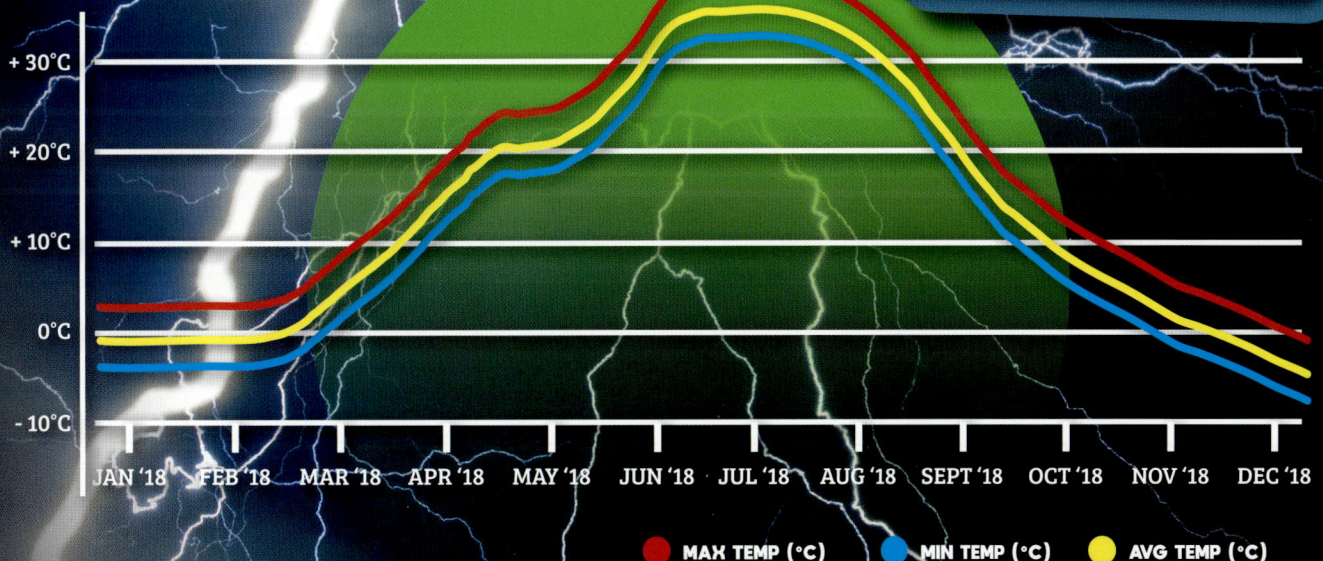

+ 30°C
+ 20°C
+ 10°C
0°C
- 10°C

JAN '18 FEB '18 MAR '18 APR '18 MAY '18 JUN '18 JUL '18 AUG '18 SEPT '18 OCT '18 NOV '18 DEC '18

● MAX TEMP (°C)   ● MIN TEMP (°C)   ● AVG TEMP (°C)

This graph shows the temperatures in Beijing, China through the year. No matter where you are in the world, temperatures are almost always warmer in summer and colder in winter.

9

WEATHER FORECAST

Sometimes it can be useful to know what the weather will be like today, tomorrow, or in a week's time, especially for people that work outside, such as farmers. **METEOROLOGISTS** use **WEATHER STATIONS** to measure things such as temperature, wind speeds and **HUMIDITY**. They can use these to track weather patterns and make **PREDICTIONS** of what the weather will be like in the future. This is called a weather forecast. Weather forecasts aren't always accurate; they don't always come true, and sometimes they might change. The Met Office forecasts weather for the UK, and they get temperature and wind speed predictions right around 90% of the time.

HOW MANY OF THE MET OFFICE'S PREDICTIONS ARE CORRECT?

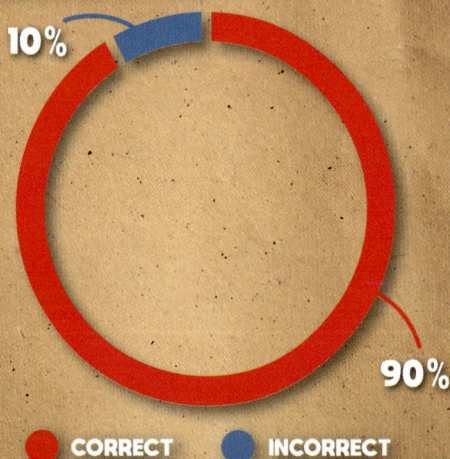

10%

90%

- CORRECT
- INCORRECT

Meteorologists record the information that they collect on a weather forecasting map. Weather maps use **ISOBARS** to show the **PRESSURE** of the air in different places. The maps also show boundaries between areas of warm air and areas of cold air. These are called fronts.

ISOBARS
WARM FRONT
COLD FRONT

Cold fronts show an area of cold, heavy air moving in and sending warm air upwards. Warm fronts show an area of warm, light air rising above colder air.

SYMBOL	WEATHER
☀	SUNNY
⛅	SUN WITH LIGHT CLOUD
🌧	HEAVY RAIN
🌨	LIGHT SNOW
☁	CLOUDY
🌬	WINDY
🌙	CLEAR NIGHT

Weather forecasts are often shown on maps or charts. Different symbols are used to represent different types of weather. A picture of the Sun shows that the weather is sunny, while a cloud with lots of raindrops means heavy rain. These symbols can be put in different places on the chart or map to show the different times or places that the weather will be felt. People can check weather forecasts online. These are usually updated regularly to keep them up to date.

These charts show the weather forecast for a day in Cape Town, South Africa, during August. The forecast shows that the temperature will reach a maximum of 17°C and the day will be mostly sunny or cloudy.

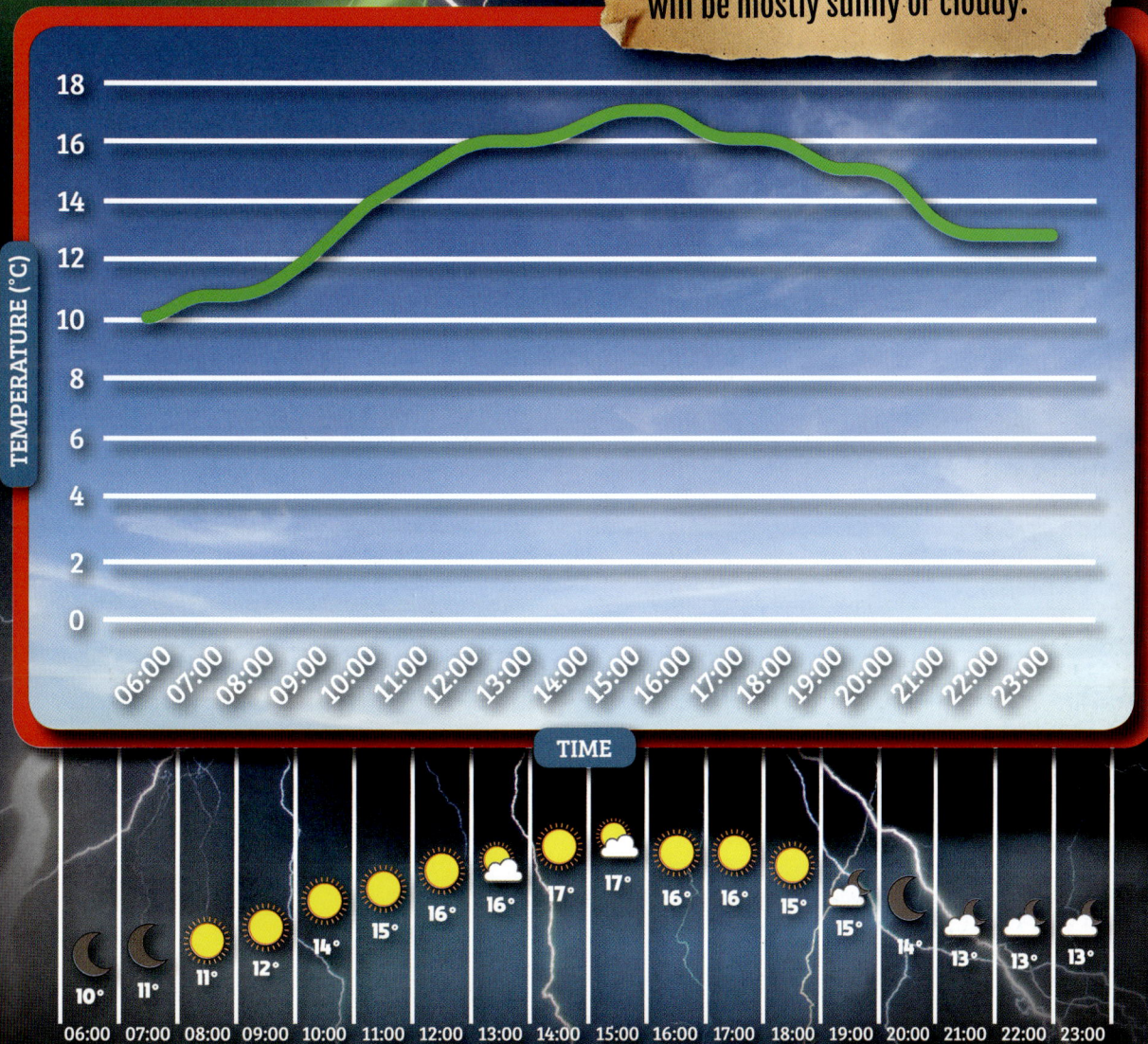

TEMPERATURE (°C)

TIME

TIME	06:00	07:00	08:00	09:00	10:00	11:00	12:00	13:00	14:00	15:00	16:00	17:00	18:00	19:00	20:00	21:00	22:00	23:00
Temp	10°	11°	11°	12°	14°	15°	16°	16°	17°	17°	16°	16°	15°	15°	14°	13°	13°	13°

CLOUDS

All clouds are formed when water vapour **CONDENSES** and changes from a gas to a liquid. Water on Earth evaporates to become water vapour. Warm air containing water vapour rises into the sky, taking the water vapour with it before cooling down. The water vapour condenses into lots of tiny water droplets, which group together to make up the clouds. Clouds can look very different to us depending on their height in the sky, the air temperature, and the amount of moisture in them. There are three main types of clouds: stratus, cumulus and cirrus.

Stratus clouds are the very lowest clouds in the sky. They often make the sky look grey.

Cirrus clouds are found very high up in the sky. They are usually long and wispy and may not even look much like clouds at all.

Cumulus clouds are white and fluffy and can be seen drifting across blue skies.

Clouds that form very high up are called high clouds, while clouds found closer to the ground are low clouds. Cirrus clouds are a type of high cloud. The air where they form is so high up that cirrus clouds are actually made from ice crystals and not water droplets. They can form up to around 12,000 m high in the sky!

HIGH CLOUDS

CIRRUS — 12,000 m

CIRROCUMULUS
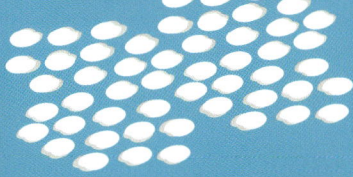

CIRROSTRATUS — 9,000 m

MIDDLE CLOUDS

CUMULONIMBUS

ALTOCUMULUS — 6,000 m

ALTOSTRATUS

LOW CLOUDS

STRATOCUMULUS

CUMULUS
 — 3,000 m

STRATUS

NIMBOSTRATUS

0 m

Sometimes, clouds might be a combination of different types of cloud. Stratocumulus clouds are a type of low cloud that have layers of stratus clouds and a surface of cumulus clouds. Stratocumulus clouds can be found around 2,000 m high in the sky and can sometimes produce light rain or drizzle.

Cumulonimbus clouds are the largest clouds in the sky. They are the only type of cloud that can produce hail, thunder and lightning.

RAIN

Clouds are made from water droplets, but sometimes these water droplets get too big and too heavy for the clouds. When this happens, the droplets fall to the ground as rain. Some water droplets are big and heavy, but others are very small and light. These small droplets are called drizzle. Large raindrops can fall as fast as 10 metres per second, but drizzle falls much slower.

2,348! 2,467!

1,714!

1,083!

853!

RAINFALL (MM)

500											
400											
300											
200											
100											
0											
JAN	FEB	MAR	APR	MAY	JUN	JUL	AUG	SEP	OCT	NOV	DEC

● ATACAMA DESERT, CHILE   ● MAWSYNRAM, INDIA

Some places receive a lot more rain than others. Mawsynram in India is one of the wettest places on Earth. Most years, it receives more than 10,000 mm of rain. That's 10 m of rain every year! The Atacama Desert in South America is one of the driest places on Earth. Only around 15 mm of rain falls per year, but during some years the desert doesn't receive any rain at all.

Rainbows are formed when sunlight shines through raindrops in the atmosphere. When the light enters the raindrop, it is **REFRACTED** and splits into the seven different colours that make up a rainbow: red, orange, yellow, green, blue, indigo and violet.

FLOODS

Sometimes, an area will receive a lot more rain than usual. If this happens suddenly, or over a long period of time, it can lead to flooding. Flooding is when there's too much water, or water in the wrong place. Some places might flood more often than others; this is usually because of what the ground is made up of. Some types of soil and rock can soak up lots of water very quickly, but others may not be able to **ABSORB** much water at all.

DROUGHTS

A drought is when a place receives a lot less rain than normal. They happen over months or even years. Droughts make the land very dry and can make it very hard to grow crops. Many people die when there isn't enough food or water to go around, and it can often take a long time for the area to **RECOVER**.

HEATWAVES

Droughts usually come after a long period of hot weather, where temperatures are much higher than the average temperature for that time of the year. If the temperature is higher than usual for at least five days in a row, it's called a heatwave. Heatwaves can either be dry, with very little or no rain, or humid, with lots of water or moisture in the atmosphere. Heatwaves can be very dangerous because they can cause our bodies to overheat, which makes us very ill.

Heatwaves are caused by slow-moving areas of high air pressure. High-pressure systems bring clear skies that allow heat from the Sun to reach Earth and warm it up. The high pressure forces air downwards and keeps warm air close to Earth's surface, which causes the temperatures to rise.

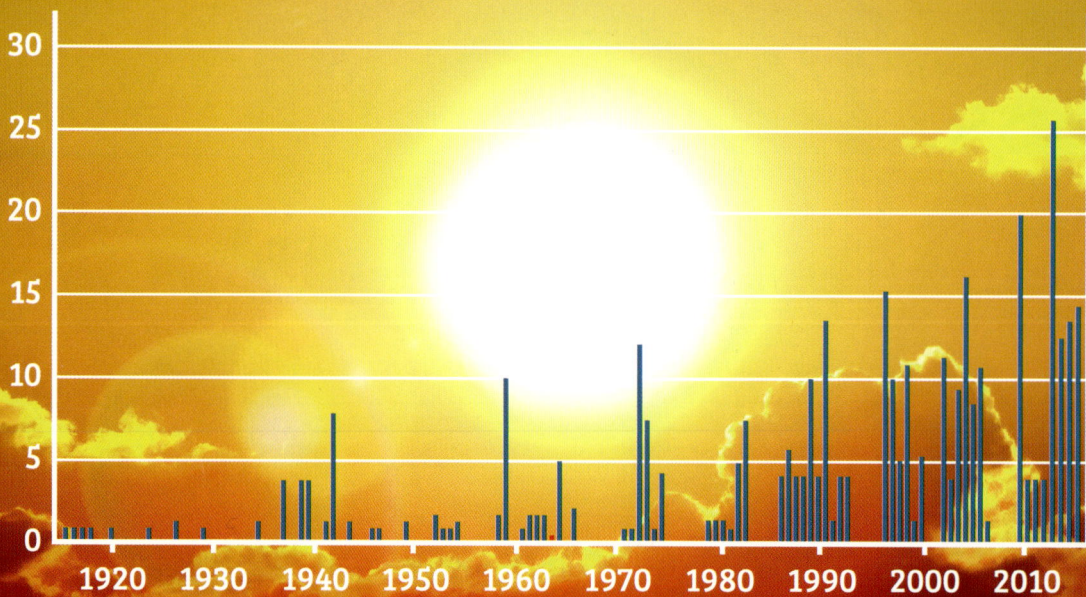

NUMBER OF EXTREME DAYS PER YEAR

30
25
20
15
10
5
0

1920   1930   1940   1950   1960   1970   1980   1990   2000   2010

Climate change is the change or changes in the world's climate over a long time. This graph shows that heatwaves in Australia are becoming more common. It has become increasingly common for periods of extreme high temperature to last for ten days or more.

Go to page 28 to read more about climate change.

WILDFIRES

Sometimes, heatwaves can lead to wildfires. Wildfires are large fires that burn through areas of bush, or grass. Heatwaves can dry out **VEGETATION** and this can cause the fire to catch and then spread very quickly. Some wildfires can burn at 800°C and spread at speeds of up to 100 m every minute.

Although wildfires usually start in **RURAL** areas, they can quickly spread to towns and cities and burn through people's homes and cars. Wildfires can be very unpredictable and are often very difficult for firefighters to control and put out. Some wildfires can burn for days, weeks, or even months before they either burn out or are **EXTINGUISHED**.

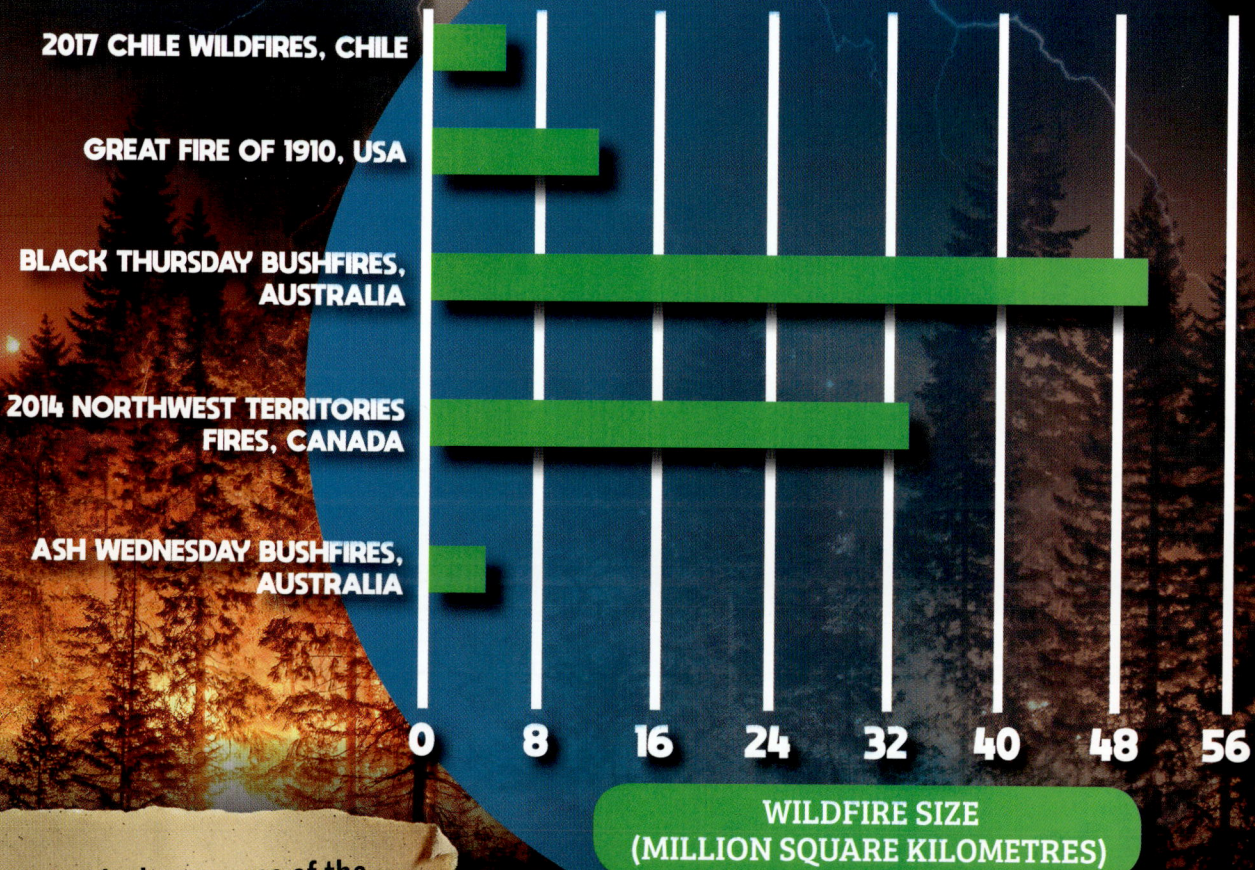

2017 CHILE WILDFIRES, CHILE

GREAT FIRE OF 1910, USA

BLACK THURSDAY BUSHFIRES, AUSTRALIA

2014 NORTHWEST TERRITORIES FIRES, CANADA

ASH WEDNESDAY BUSHFIRES, AUSTRALIA

0   8   16   24   32   40   48   56

WILDFIRE SIZE (MILLION SQUARE KILOMETRES)

This graph shows some of the largest wildfires on Earth. The Black Thursday bushfires swept through over 48,000 **SQUARE KILOMETRES** in Victoria, Australia in 1851. 12 people, one million sheep and thousands of cattle died in the fires.

COLD SPELLS

Summer is the best time for going to the beach and playing out in the sun. But what about winter? Winter is much colder than summer, and in some places it might even snow. High up in the Arctic Circle near the North Pole, winters are long and dark. Because of the Earth's tilt, the North Pole is in almost complete darkness from October until March.

Like the Arctic, Antarctica spends around half of the year in darkness and half of the year in continuous sunlight. However, because it is in the Southern Hemisphere, Antarctica's winter is from around February until October. During its winter, Antarctica is the coldest place on Earth. Scientists used satellites to record a temperature of -98°C, and they don't believe Earth can get much colder than this.

0°C – TEMPERATURE THAT WATER FREEZES AT

Penguins have lots of feathers and a thick layer of fat that helps them to stay warm and survive the cold temperatures in Antarctica. Humans don't have these **ADAPTATIONS**, so people working in Antarctica have to wear lots of thick clothes and stay inside when it gets too cold.

TEMPERATURE (°C)

0
-10
-20
-30
-40
-50
-60
-70
-80
-90
-100

-98°C – THE COLDEST TEMPERATURE ON EARTH

If you've been outside on a very cold day, you might have noticed that the ground beneath your feet can be a bit slippery. This is caused by rain and drizzle that freezes and turns to ice when it lands on a very cold surface. Ice can form over roads and paths, and even lakes and rivers if the water is cold enough.

Scientists use ice to learn more about Earth's history. Long tubes of ice called ice cores can be drilled from thick ice sheets near to the North and South Poles. Ice cores have layers that can be counted up to work out how old the ice is. The different layers can also be studied to show us things about the climate during a certain year or period in history.

When water drips slowly from somewhere high up and freezes solid, it can form beautiful, hanging spikes of ice called icicles. Icicles can form on trees, bridges, houses and road signs.

The thickest section of ice ever recorded was found in Antarctica in 1975. Scientists measured the ice and found it to be over 4.7 kilometres (km) thick!

SNOW

Snowflakes are tiny water droplets that freeze to become ice crystals. Some snowflakes are made up of several water droplets that freeze together, and others are formed when water droplets collect and freeze around a small piece of dust or pollen. Although snowflakes might all look very similar, each one is **UNIQUE**. Every snowflake is different, and their shape depends on the temperature and humidity of the air when they form. Most snowflakes are either plate snowflakes or column snowflakes. The most recognised snowflake shape is a dendrite snowflake, which is a type of plate snowflake. Dendrite snowflakes have six branches and their name means 'tree-like'.

This graph shows how temperature and humidity affect the different types of snowflake that form.

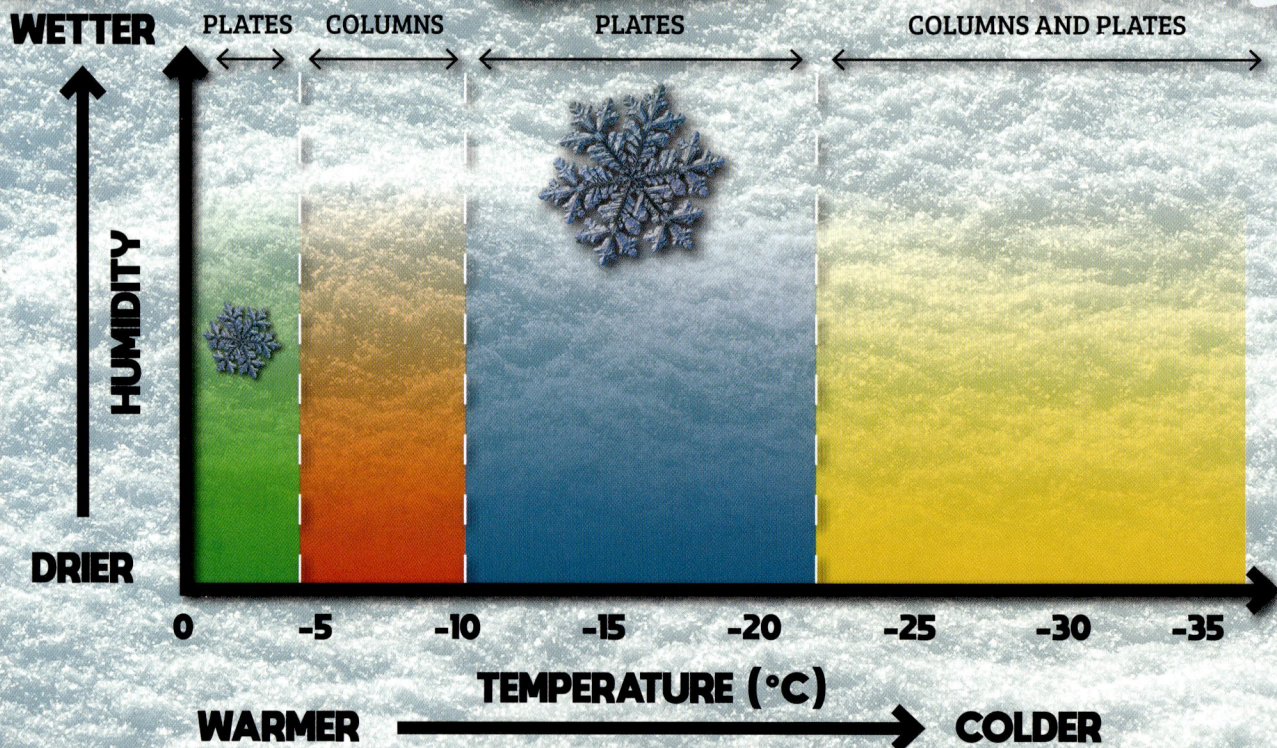

| WETTER | PLATES | COLUMNS | PLATES | COLUMNS AND PLATES |

HUMIDITY

DRIER

| 0 | -5 | -10 | -15 | -20 | -25 | -30 | -35 |

TEMPERATURE (°C)

WARMER → COLDER

The two snowflakes on this graph are dendrite snowflakes. Dendrite snowflakes can form at different temperatures and at different levels of humidity.

In some places on Earth, if the air temperature gets below 2°C, snowflakes will bunch together and fall from the sky as snow. Snow can be fun for playing in and making snowmen. If a lot of snow falls, it can completely cover roads and buildings and make it very difficult for people to get around. Public transport might be delayed, and flights may even be **GROUNDED** if the snow is very heavy or deep.

Every year, many people in the UK hope for a 'white Christmas'. This is when snow falls on Christmas Day. However, white Christmases are very rare as, on average, it only snows on a maximum of four days in December in the UK.

NUMBER OF WEATHER STATIONS ACROSS THE UK THAT REPORTED SNOW ON THE GROUND

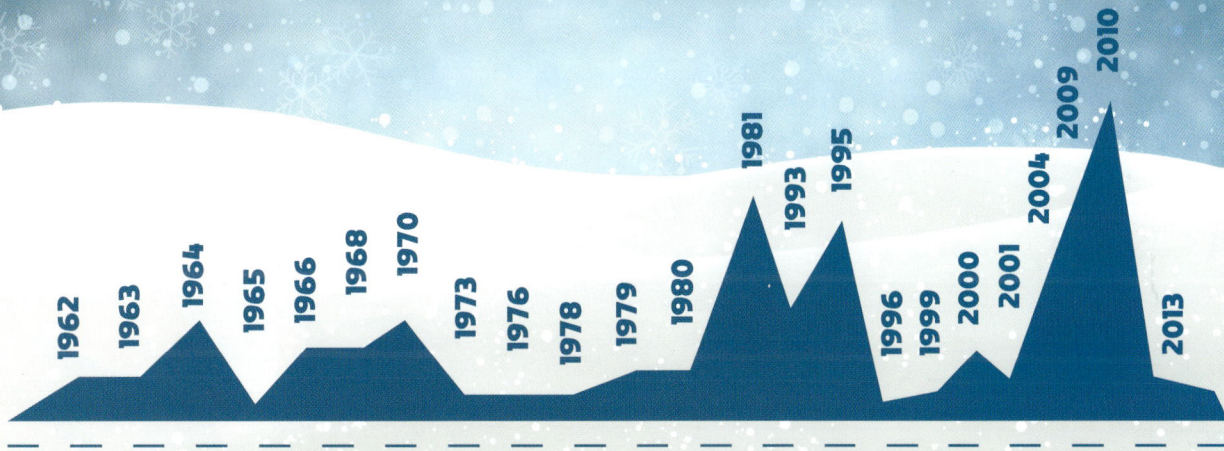

1962 1963 1964 1965 1966 1968 1970 1973 1976 1978 1979 1980 1981 1993 1995 1996 1999 2000 2001 2004 2009 2010 2013

This line graph shows the years when the most weather stations reported having snow on the ground on Christmas Day.

AURORAS

The Sun affects our weather by giving us heat and light, but it also sends strong solar winds up into space and towards Earth. Solar wind is made up of lots of **CHARGED PARTICLES**. These particles bounce off a magnetic field that surrounds Earth. However, sometimes the Sun shoots up solar flares that give the particles enough energy to crash into the magnetic field. When this happens, the particles collide with the gases in Earth's atmosphere to produce different coloured lights, called auroras. In the Northern Hemisphere, the lights are called the northern lights, or aurora borealis. In the Southern Hemisphere, the lights are called the southern lights, or aurora australis.

STRENGTH OF SOLAR FLARES

- LOWEST
- LOW
- HIGH
- HIGHEST

The northern lights are usually only visible in and around the Arctic Circle. This graph shows how strong solar flares from the Sun must be to see the northern lights in different parts of the Northern Hemisphere.

When solar wind particles collide with oxygen, they produce a green or red light. When they collide with nitrogen, blue or purple lights are produced.

Earth isn't the only planet that has auroras. Scientists have spotted auroras on Saturn and Jupiter that are caused by solar winds, just like our auroras on Earth. In fact, any planet that has an atmosphere and a magnetic field will probably have an aurora.

Like on Earth, Jupiter's auroras are produced when charged particles collide with the planet's atmosphere. These charged particles come from the Sun, but they also come from one of Jupiter's moons named Io. As Io orbits Jupiter, charged particles are thrown into space towards Jupiter's magnetic field. These particles combine with gases in the planet's atmosphere and produce red, green or purple auroras depending on what the gases are.

In total, scientists believe that Jupiter has 79 moons. Jupiter's four largest moons are called the Galilean moons, or Galilean satellites, because they were discovered by the Italian astronomer Galileo Galilei in 1610.

WAVE LENGTH (NANOMETRES)

700
600
580
550
475
450
400

RADIO WAVES

MICROWAVES

INFRARED

VISIBLE LIGHT

ULTRAVIOLET

X-RAYS

GAMMA RAYS

All these waves make up something called the electromagnetic spectrum.

There are many different types of light in the electromagnetic spectrum, but humans can only see some of this light – this is called visible light. Saturn's auroras can only be seen in ultraviolet light, which makes them invisible to us. They are only visible from space using special equipment.

STORMS

Thunderstorms form in large cumulonimbus clouds when water droplets inside the cloud combine with warm air. This can produce winds of over 160 kilometres per hour (kph), bright flashes of lightning and loud, rumbling claps of thunder. Heavy rain or hail usually comes with a thunderstorm too.

If a cumulonimbus cloud is very cold, the water droplets inside it turn to ice. These ice droplets can knock against each other and produce electricity. The electricity builds up until it is released into the atmosphere as lightning. Lightning bolts can be up to 6 km long and reach temperatures of 30,000°C – that's five times hotter than the surface of the Sun! Lightning makes the surrounding air very hot very quickly, which makes the air suddenly spread out. This causes the rumbling sounds of thunder.

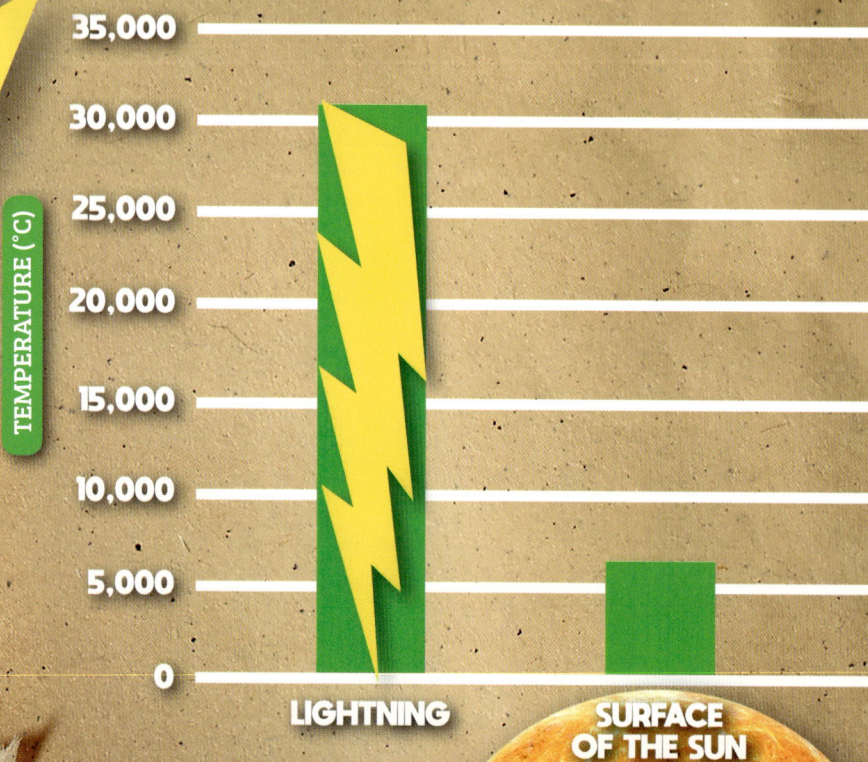

TEMPERATURE (°C)

35,000
30,000
25,000
20,000
15,000
10,000
5,000
0

LIGHTNING

SURFACE OF THE SUN

Tropical storms are large storms that form over warm oceans in the tropical areas of Earth, near to the Equator. They begin as small storms, but as warm, moist air rises from the surface of the ocean, the storms get bigger and bigger until they're huge, spinning clouds of wind and rain. At the centre of each tropical storm is a very calm area. This is called the eye of the storm and tropical storms rotate around their eye. Some eyes, like the eye of Hurricane Wilma in 2005, are quite small, while others, like the eye of Typhoon Carmen in 1960, are very big.

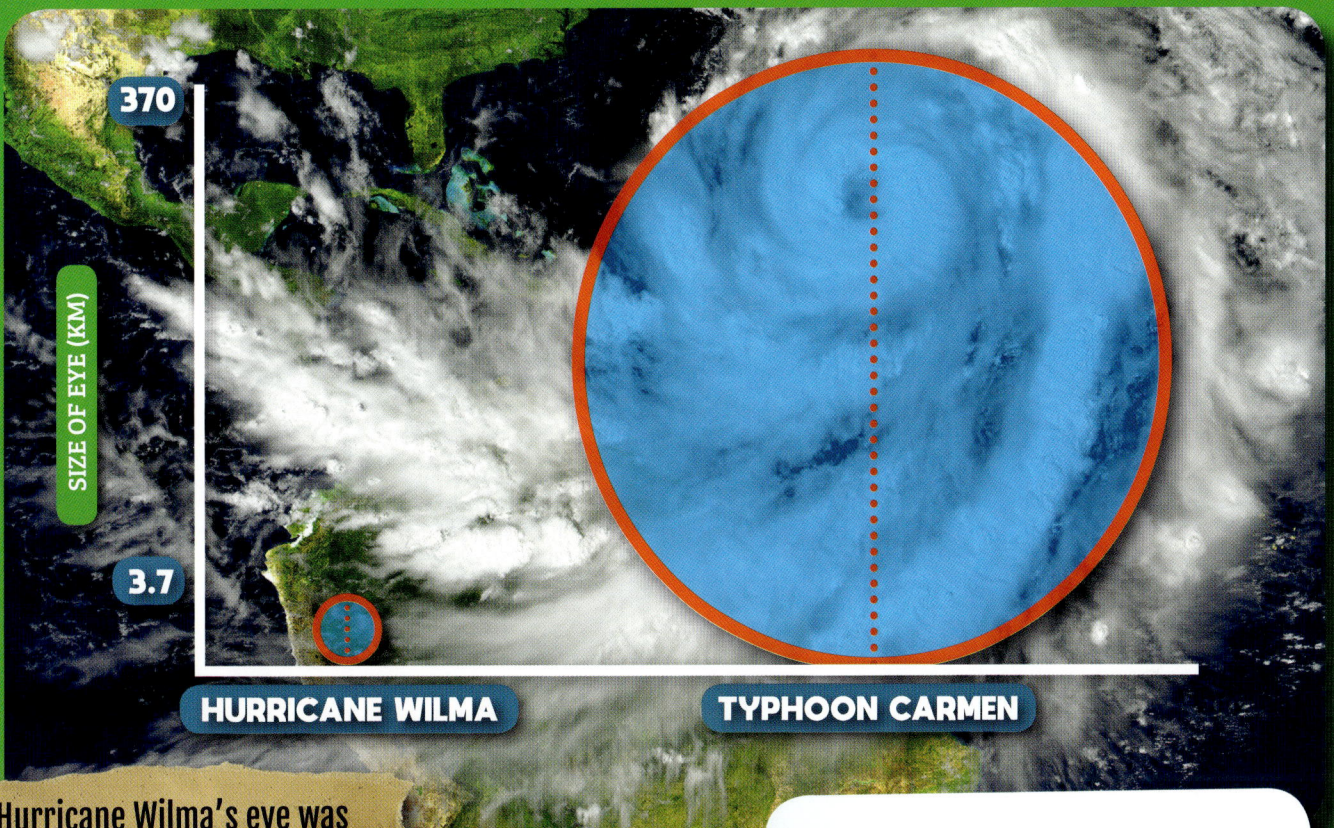

SIZE OF EYE (KM)

370

3.7

HURRICANE WILMA

TYPHOON CARMEN

Hurricane Wilma's eye was around 3.7 km in diameter, whereas Typhoon Carmen's eye had a diameter of 370 km – that's 100 times bigger!

It can often take many years and a lot of money to repair the damage caused by a tropical storm. In August 2005, a hurricane called Hurricane Katrina hit the US. The hurricane caused a **STORM SURGE** that flooded 80% of the city of New Orleans. More than 90 countries offered money, supplies or volunteers to help with the aftermath of the disaster.

Depending on where in the world and over which ocean a tropical storm forms, it is called either a hurricane, cyclone, or a typhoon.

TORNADOES

When warm air meets cold air inside a storm cloud, that air can move upwards very quickly. Winds blowing from different directions can then make the cloud spin around and rotate. A long funnel of air may drop from the cloud towards the ground. This is called a tornado. Tornadoes can be very narrow or very wide. Some only last for a few seconds, while others can last for more than an hour.

The winds inside a tornado can reach speeds of up to 480 kph. That's fast and strong enough to pull trees up from the ground, rip roofs off houses and throw cars hundreds of metres. Sometimes, a tornado might pick something up, such as a car, travel a distance of up to 10 km and then 'spit' it out.

	ENHANCED FUJITA SCALE
EF−0	LIGHT DAMAGE
EF−1	MODERATE DAMAGE
EF−2	CONSIDERABLE DAMAGE
EF−3	SEVERE DAMAGE
EF−4	DEVASTATING DAMAGE
EF−5	INCREDIBLE DAMAGE

Tornadoes are rated using the Enhanced Fujita Scale (or EF-Scale), which groups tornadoes based on how strong they are and how much damage they cause.

BELOW EF-3

EF-3 AND ABOVE

This pie chart shows the **PROPORTION** of tornadoes in the US every year that are weak (below EF-3) and violent (EF-3 and above). Only around 5% of all tornadoes that occur in the US are violent tornadoes, but these are the ones that cause the most damage.

TORNADO ALLEY

Although tornadoes can occur almost anywhere in the world, the US sees more tornadoes than any other country on Earth. More than 1,200 tornadoes hit the US every year, and most of these occur in an area called Tornado Alley. Tornado Alley is located in the **MIDWEST** of the US, where warm, moist air from the Gulf of Mexico meets cold air moving south from Canada to produce lots of thunderstorms.

Supercells are large thunderstorms that contain a **VORTEX** of fast-spinning, rising air called a mesocyclone. Supercells can produce hail, fast winds, heavy rain, lightning and violent tornadoes. Supercell thunderstorms can hit Tornado Alley at any time, but they are most common in spring, with most tornadoes occurring in May.

This graph shows how the number of tornadoes reported in the US between 1950 and 2010 has increased. This is due to modern weather equipment and more people living in the US to spot them.

U.S. ANNUAL TORNADO COUNT

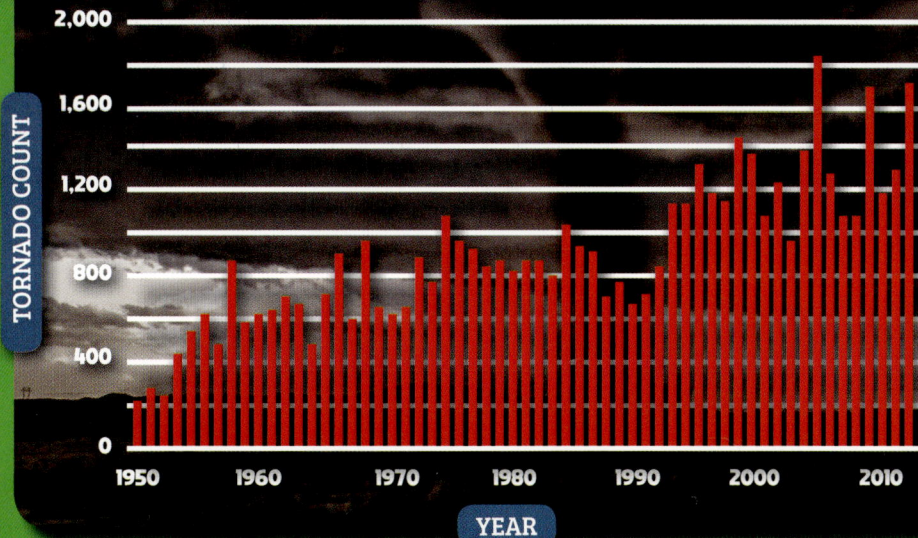

TORNADO COUNT

2,000

1,600

1,200

800

400

0

1950   1960   1970   1980   1990   2000   2010

YEAR

CLIMATE CHANGE

Climate change is the way Earth's climate is changing over a period of time. Over the past 100 years, Earth's average surface temperature has risen by almost 1°C. This is called global warming, and it's just one way that our climate is changing.

Humans are the main cause of climate change. All over the world we burn fossil fuels such as oil and gas to power our cars and heat our homes. Burning oil and gas releases greenhouse gases into the atmosphere. These gases surround Earth like a blanket and trap heat from the Sun. This warms Earth up in a process called the greenhouse effect. As the climate continues to change and Earth warms up even more, extreme weather such as hurricanes and tornadoes could become more common. The warmer temperatures could also bring longer droughts and more frequent wildfires, but no one knows for sure exactly how the world will be affected.

GLOBAL AVERAGE TEMPERATURE (°C) – 5 YEAR AVERAGE

Values on vertical axis: 13.5, 13.6, 13.7, 13.8, 13.9, 14.0, 14.1, 14.2, 14.3, 14.4

Values on horizontal axis: 1860, 1880, 1900, 1920, 1940, 1960, 1980, 2000

YEAR

Global warming is causing the ice caps to melt. Animals such as polar bears and seals are in danger of losing their habitats completely if global warming continues.

Carbon dioxide CO_2 is a greenhouse gas. However, this doesn't mean that it's bad. The greenhouse gases keep Earth warm and without them, our planet would be far too cold to live on. CO_2 can be found in our atmosphere and in the air around us. Animals **EXHALE** CO_2 and plants absorb it. This keeps the level of CO_2 in our atmosphere balanced and stops Earth from getting too hot or too cold.

As humans burn more fossil fuels, more CO_2 enters our atmosphere and adds to the greenhouse effect. There is now more CO_2 in our atmosphere than ever before. To prevent even more CO_2 being released, many people are beginning to use **RENEWABLE ENERGY SOURCES** instead of fossil fuels, which can then be **CONVERTED** into electricity. This includes energy from the Sun, wind and oceans.

CARBON DIOXIDE LEVEL (PARTS PER MILLION)

| 500 |
| 480 |
| 460 |
| 440 |
| 420 |
| 400 |
| 380 |
| 360 |
| 340 |
| 320 |
| 300 |
| 280 |
| 260 |
| 240 |
| 220 |
| 200 |
| 180 |
| 160 |

400,000   350,000   300,000   250,000   200,000   150,000   100,000   50,000   0

YEARS BEFORE TODAY
(0 = 1950)

● CURRENT LEVEL
● 1950 LEVEL

ACTIVITY: GET SMART!

DAY	MY WEATHER FORECAST		ACTUAL WEATHER	
MONDAY	20°C	☀	23°C	☀
TUESDAY	22°C	⛅	21°C	⛅
WEDNESDAY	23°C	☀	19°C	☁
THURSDAY	18°C	🌧	21°C	⛅
FRIDAY	20°C	⛅	20°C	⛅

Have a go at being a meteorologist and come up with your very own weather forecasts. Do you think it will be sunny or cloudy? Will it rain or snow? Maybe there'll be a thunderstorm! Record all of your predictions in a table and compare them with what the weather is actually like on each day. How close were your predictions?

You can put all of the temperatures on a bar chart or line graph. What does your graph look like?

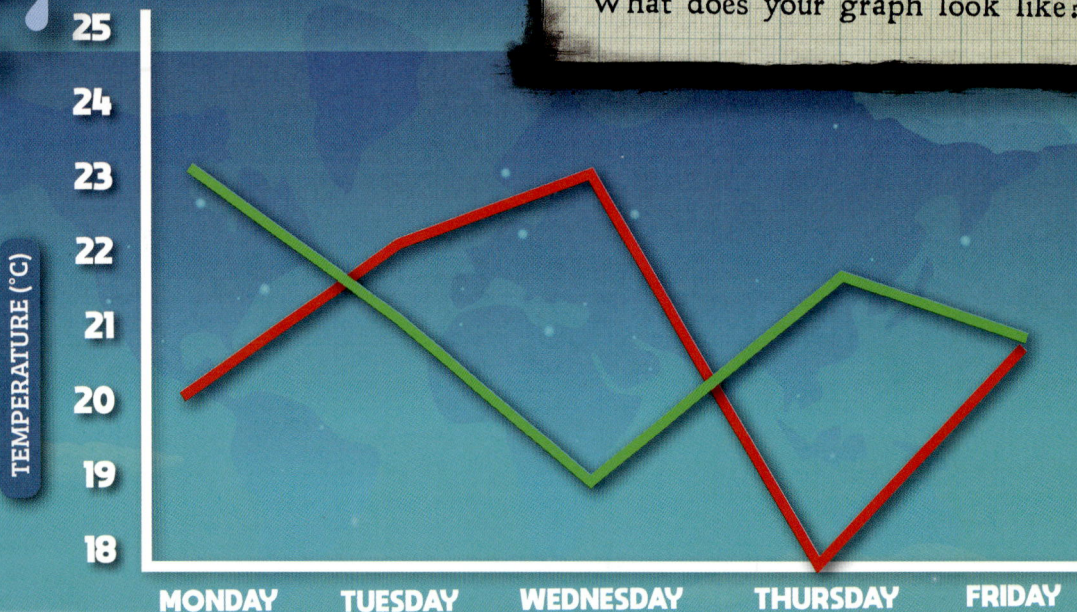

TEMPERATURE (°C)

MONDAY TUESDAY WEDNESDAY THURSDAY FRIDAY

DAY

— MY WEATHER FORECAST
— ACTUAL WEATHER

GLOSSARY

ABSORB	to take in or soak up
ADAPTATIONS	changes or characteristics that occur over time to suit different conditions
ATMOSPHERE	the mixture of gases that make up the air and surround the Earth
AVERAGE	the typical amount or most central number of a range of numbers
CHARGED PARTICLES	an atom or something smaller with an electric charge
CONDENSES	changes from a gas or vapour into a liquid
CONVERTED	to be changed from one form of something to another
EXHALE	breathe out
EXTINGUISHED	put out
GASES	air-like substances that expand freely to fill any space available
GROUNDED	stopped from flying
HUMIDITY	amount of water vapour in the air
INTERPRET	to understand or work out
ISOBARS	lines on a map that join together places with the same pressure
METEOROLOGISTS	scientists who study weather
MIDWEST	a region in the US in the north of the country
MILD	not extremely hot; warm or temperate
MOISTURE	liquid in the form of very small drops
POSITIVE CORRELATION	a relationship between two sets of data where they increase or decrease together
PREDICTABLE	not unusual; able to be predicted or guessed
PREDICTIONS	things that someone has guessed will happen in the future
PRESSURE	a continuous physical force exerted on an object, which is caused by something pressing against it
PROPORTION	a share of something in relation to the whole
RECOVER	return to normal
REFRACTED	what happens to a ray of light when it passes through something that changes its speed
RENEWABLE ENERGY SOURCES	sources of energy that do not run out when used
RURAL	relating to or characteristic of the countryside
SQUARE KILOMETRES	a measurement of an area that is a square with each side being a kilometre in length
STORM SURGE	when the sea rises due to a storm or winds
UNIQUE	being the only one of its kind
VEGETATION	plants found in a particular area or plants considered collectively
VORTEX	a spinning mass of air or liquid, such as a whirlpool or whirlwind
WEATHER STATIONS	places where weather conditions are measured

INDEX